How do you do it?

30 Day Devotional for Special Needs Mommas

By: Christina Herzog
Edited by: Belinda Rohling Padgett

Dedication Page

I want to dedicate this book to a few people. First and foremost this book is for my husband. He is fighting the daily fight with me and supports me in every way.

I also want to dedicate this to my wonderful parents. They have been there for me and supported me in my struggle.

Lastly, I want to dedicate this book to my children. They are my inspiration and the reason that I do what I do.

Preface

Ten balloons dangling off the shopping cart loaded with one child in the cart and one in the baby seat. Two more kids follow behind me like little jumping beans hopping and wiggling around the cart but staying at a close proximity. One child begging for candy, another asking to go buy laundry detergent, the baby desperately attempting to stand up and break free from the restraints of the shopping cart buckle. Then my poor eight year old with both hands over his ears looking stressed. Then a lady walks by and says," Wow I do not know how you do it?" I just smile and keep walking. This lady doesn't even know the half of it. Yes, we have four children but you cannot tell by looking at us but two of my children also have been diagnosed with autism.

As a mom of children and a mom of autistic children, I constantly get asked the question "how do you do it?" Not to mention I have a husband that works a lot and I also used to work a full time job as a middle school teacher. I am not sure if people are impressed or if they just think I am crazy. Obviously, I did not ask to be an autism mom. I did not ask to raise autistic children but that is what happened. I live everyday trying to care for children on and off the spectrum. My typical answer when asked this question is God. The only reason I keep going is God. I get up early before children to read my Bible and devotionals, I watch different preachers on TV, and I listen to a lot of Christian music. In order to survive autism, I need constant encouragement. I need God to survive this. I cannot do anything without God. I have an ongoing conversation with God almost all day not because I feel like I am super religious, but because I need God. I need his comfort and his encouragement just to make it to bedtime. I basically have to surround myself with Godly things to stay calm.

I decided to write this book to share how I am surviving autism as a Christian mom. I have felt God pushing me to share my life story with others to hopefully inspire other special needs moms to stay strong in the Lord. I want to share my secret to being content and calm in the stressful life I have been blessed with. I am going to share verses that give me hope and understanding. Be warned though, there will be stories of poop, spit, and maybe some disturbing behavior, but this is our life.

DAY 1:

Every good and perfect gift is from above, coming down from the Father of the heavenly lights, who does not change like shifting shadows.
James 1:17

I open my son's door to a strong, familiar smell of poop again. This was the third time this week that he decided to not only poop in his room at night but to smear it all over his bed, walls, and dresser. My husband jokingly refer to this as "fun with feces." This has become a common occurrence in our household. It has even gotten to the point where we both just jump into a cleaning role. One of us grabs our eight year old to get him in the shower, while the other person starts the exciting task of cleaning poop off everything in his room. Definitely not what either of us expected when we became parents. The gift we seem to have is much stinkier than we expected.

There was a time in my life when I thought that I could control everything. I remember being pregnant with my first child and I had this dream of this "perfect child." Being a football mom and attending awards ceremony was the plan. In my mind, my child was going to be good at everything. He would be an Honor student, good at sports, and have lots of friends. It wasn't long after my first child was born that reality set in.

My first two children both were diagnosed with autism. My dreams of a "perfect child" was gone and there was no hope of ever having this child that I thought I wanted. Obviously, my heart was broken. I almost felt like I was mourning the loss of this "perfect child" dream. I was not sure what I did to deserve not one but two children with autism. I watched my friends and family members get my dream children. I couldn't help but feel angry. I prayed and prayed that God would somehow fix my children into the perfect dream children that I wanted until I stumbled upon this verse.

It was then that I realized my children weren't broken, they were good and perfect in God's eyes. He made them for me and trusted me to care for his small masterpieces. Instead of seeing how perfect they were, I was complaining. My sweet boys were not made to be my dream, but they were made perfectly the way that God intended. They were wild flowers in a world full of roses. They are beautiful, just in a world that didn't recognize their beauty.

I have stopped praying for God to create my "perfect child." God already created his perfect child and I have been entrusted to care for his perfect children. I have learned to appreciate the masterpieces that God has given me.

Daily Challenge

Think of things that make your child perfect in God's eyes and thank God for the perfect child that he has given you despite the challenges that face you both.

DAY 2

***I praise you because I am fearfully and wonderfully made; your works are wonderful, I know that full well.
Psalm 139:14***

"Can I please carry the fabric softener to the car?" Jayden excitedly squeals. My 10 year old begged to come to the store with me. I decided to let him not realizing that his goal was for me to purchase some fabric softener. The cashier smiled at him and handed him the blue bottle of fabric softener. My son then starts telling her that we need fabric softener for our front load washing machine and that it will make our clothes smell good. He then begins interrogating her about her washing machine. Everybody typically smiles and answers his questions but I can see the look of confusion in their eye. My 10 year old continues to ask a million questions without ever noticing that people find it strange. You can tell they are trying to figure out why my 10 year old son wants to discuss the agitator in the washer or the pros and cons of a front loader versus a top loader. He could probably discuss washing machines for hours. He spends his days either washing our laundry or watching Youtube videos about washing machines. He is completely obsessed.

This is not his first obsession. We tend to go through phases of obsessions. At one point it was the weather then air conditioners and fans. The list could go on. He gets on a kick and that is the household conversation for weeks or months. Definitely, not what you'd expect from a 10 year old boy. Most of our family and friends have come to enjoy these conversations and love his unique personality.

When he was little, I remember being sad that he was autistic. As he has gotten older, I have started to realize that he is such a blessing. God shows me every day that he knew what he was doing when he made Jayden. Jayden is a beautiful child. Not everybody recognizes how wonderful he is but he is a beautiful, wonderful child of God. I praise God every day for sending me my unique boy. I pray that my son continues to be his own person. At the age of 10, he already recognizes his talents and he does not care what anybody thinks.

I think as a special needs parent, I have to remind myself that my children are wonderfully made despite the fact that the world sees them as disabled or different. If I spend time in my day praising God for their beautiful uniqueness, it makes me appreciate their qualities and focus on the things that they are capable of doing. They really are amazing boys.

Daily Challenge:

Thank God for all of the ways that your child is unique. Sometimes being unique is not seen as a positive in this world but when I look at my children, I can see that they are not like anybody else. My boys are their own unique people and they have no fear of being their own people.

DAY 3

As the heavens are higher than the earth, so are my ways higher than your ways and my thoughts than your thoughts.
Isaiah 55:9

The room was crowded and loud. Not only were people talking but they had music playing. Isaac's little hands went over his ears. I knew this was the first step to a meltdown but I pushed on. A nice lady had us follow her to a desk and started asking questions about my children's names and ages. Isaac pushed his hands tighter over his ears and I could feel his anxiety level rising. Then his pretty blue eyes make perfect eye contact with me. I can tell he will not make it much longer but this person keeps asking questions. "Want to go bye bye," Isaac says in a loud, anxious voice. I hug him and tell him that we are almost done. Then my sweet boy grabs my hair and proceeds to latch on to attempt to bang his head against my head. This is Isaac's signature move when he gets overstimulated. I manage to get my head free from his death grip for him to turn to my one year old and try to get her also. I managed to save both of us from his wrath. With crazy hair and tears in my eyes, I tell the church lady that we were just going to leave. Obviously, we would be unable to go to church. At this point, I think she realized that we did not have time for more questions and she took us to the sensory room. Isaac immediately calmed down. He found a ball and starts bouncing around the room. I finally made it to the adult service and I plopped in the chair from exhaustion but I made it.

As I sat there in church, I started to wonder "why me?" I am literally getting beat up by an eight year old. I was embarrassed and hurt yet I have no control to change anything. Sometimes I feel like I am just holding on for dear life because things feel so out of control. The words to the worship song brought tears to my eyes. I raised my hands and just poured my heart into worship. Sometimes putting the problems aside and just singing remind me that we serve a good father. There is no way that I can comprehend why things are the way they are. The best thing we can do is to accept life and trust that God knows what he is doing. I have to remind myself constantly that God's ways are higher than my own. I have no idea why I have 2 autistic children or if they will ever get better but I do know that God has plan. My life and my children are a small piece in God's puzzle. He is God and I am not. It is not my job to figure out why I was blessed with living in the world of autism. It is my job to trust that God knows what he is doing.

Daily Challenge

Make a list of things that you need to trust God for. Stop trying to figure everything out. Take your list and start praying to God not to just fix everything but to be content despite the problems.

DAY 4

And we know that in all things God works for the good of those who love him, who have been called according to his purpose.

Romans 8:28

I learned this verse long before I ever became an autism mom. I was in 4th grade when I first read this verse. I actually saw this verse in the newspaper right after the church I attended caught on fire. A huge portion of the church burnt down. I just remember being so impressed that the church suffered this huge tragedy and they still trusted God. I also remember being impressed that the newspaper posted a Bible verse.

I've depended on this verse a lot during my years of being an autism mom. From the horrible moment sitting in the meeting when they told us that Jayden was autistic and then 2 years later finding out Isaac was also autistic all the way up to the IEP meetings with no progress made, seeing the state test scores, no birthday invites, and still not hearing my sweet boy call me mom. In some ways I felt so cheated that I was missing out on the normal parenting things but somewhere in all of this God is working for our good. He has a plan greater than any plan I could ever create. He is creating a masterpiece out of us and we just cannot see the big picture. At this point in my life, I feel like my only option is to trust God and trust that he has something bigger at work that is beyond my understanding.

I will admit though when I talk to an 8 year old, I always think that's what he should be doing. It makes me sad and I can't help but wonder. "*Hey, God it says here all things work for good. How can having 2 autistic children be good?*" I'm not saying I never doubt but I read this verse and it is hung up at my house as a reminder that something good will come out of this. There is a purpose and a reason behind God's plan.

Daily Challenge

Today I challenge you to think of something that has come out of your situation. I do have 2 children with autism but many good things have come out of my situation. I am a stronger and more patient person. I am also more understanding of others. I used to be too judgmental of others and having children with autism makes me look at others differently. I am slower to judge and quicker to be understanding. I also feel that I have met so many wonderful people that I only met because of my kids.

DAY 5

Consider it pure joy, my brothers and sisters, whenever you face trials of many kinds, because you know that the testing of your faith produces perseverance.
James 1:2-3

The bouncy ball is banging across the floor and Isaac squeals joyfully around his room. It sounds a lot like an NBA game in his room right now as he thuds back and forth bouncing his ball and jumping from his bed to his air mattress. Every few minutes he releases a loud happy sound. He echoes throughout the silent house of sleeping kids. I love hearing his happy sounds, I just wish they did not come at 4:30 AM. Ironically, this is sleeping in for him. He is notorious for getting up at 2 AM and 3 AM some mornings. Getting him to sleep at night is also a task. I am not quite sure how he is so happy in the morning since he probably average 4 or 5 hours of sleep. I have had people say that I should just let him play in his room and keep sleeping but if I do that, then we are back to cleaning poop and/or pee.

I will be honest when I have to get up at 4 AM, I do not feel very joyful. When I have to scrub poop from the carpet, I do not feel joyful. When my son has a meltdown and starts attacking me, I do not feel joyful. I do believe that I am definitely learning a lot and at this point in my autism journey, I probably have a lot of perseverance. I will be honest, I do not feel strong until somebody else points out how hard my life is. I do not even think about how hard it is, I just do it. I think if I sat around thinking about how hard it is, then I would not be able to do it. Instead, I just ask God for strength and thank God for another day with my babies.

This experience has also increased my faith. I find myself depending on God a lot more than I ever did before I had children. I trust that God is planning something great for my family. I have no clue what it is but I have faith that something great is coming. When I keep my eyes on God and just keep going, then I feel content but I do get down sometimes. I can feel when I start slipping from God because I start feeling sorry for myself. I would say that my biggest defense to self pity is surrounding myself with Godly things. I watch preachers on TV, I worship to Christian music, and I read my Bible. These things calm my soul and help me get perspective. I know that my struggles are teaching me perseverance and my faith is stronger than ever because of my struggles.

Daily Challenge

I challenge you today to think about and list out some of the trials that you have overcome already. Sometimes, I look back at what I have already overcome and it helps strengthen my faith. At one point in my life, I had 3 boys (2 with autism) all 3 years old and younger, all in diapers and I survived. I potty trained 2 autistic boys! I face new challenges daily but when I look at what God has already helped me through it makes me feel empowered and gives me strength to keep trusting God for my new problems.

<u>DAY 6</u>

Therefore I tell you, whatever you ask for in prayer, believe that you have received it, and it will be yours.
Mark 11:24

The swaying back and forth actually seems to be moving the entire car. The distressed look in his eyes and the tears have started falling from his face. His hands clenched tightly over his ears to block all sounds. We are all trapped in the car as Isaac's meltdown starts to unfold. Even my 4 year old seems to know the signs. He tries to console and stop the meltdown but it is already too late. Meltdowns in the car are probably the scariest because I cannot protect my other kids from the wrath of Isaac. Instead of getting upset, I told my other boys that we were going to pray. We all started praying that God would help Isaac calm down so we could get to Grandpa's house.

Within a few minutes of our family prayer, Isaac started to calm down. He stopped swaying and took his hands off of his ears. I was so relieved that the prayer worked. Sometimes I forget that God answers all prayers, even the small ones. I tend to focus on begging God to fix my children but I forget that God can help me with the small stuff too. I thank God that he answers the small prayers.

We have lots of tiny miracles at our house every day. When God calms a meltdown or when Isaac remembers to use his words instead of attack or meltdown. As an autism momma, you learn to celebrate the small miracles. Every little accomplishment is one step closer to healing. Some of my miracles are not things most people would get excited about but again I think when you have children with special needs, your perspective changes. You learn to appreciate every little thing and you do not take for granted the many blessings that you've been given.

When my daughter was a one year old, she really liked pennies but when I took them away she would fall on the floor and scream. I know taking the penny away did not make her happy but I also know that if I let her keep the penny then she would most likely choke on it or swallow it. I think God works the same way. Sometimes, we really want a pretty penny but

God knows that it is not the time for us to have the pretty penny so he says no. Just like my daughter, we sometimes throw a fit and beg but God knows what is best for us even if we cannot comprehend why.

Despite my prayers, God has not taken away the autism from my boys. He has not healed them and they still are not neurotypical. I think we have to remember though that God cannot do everything we say. He is not a genie in a bottle that just answers your wishes. Unfortunately, sometimes the answer is no or maybe later. God is our father so sometimes he has to say no to protect us or because he has a bigger plan.

Daily Challenge

Can you think of any prayers that you are glad God didn't give you what you wanted? I always think back to that Garth Brooks song about him praying to be with a girl and it doesn't work out but he is thankful because he found the love of his life. Do you have any unanswered prayers that you can thank God for not answering? Try to think of a few and thank God for saying no sometimes.

DAY 7

But seek first his kingdom and his righteousness,
and all these things will be given to you as well.
Matthew 6: 33

"Mommy, I don't think I need any Jesus today" was my 10 year old's response when I told him to get ready for church. I couldn't help but giggle at his response. I love how he uses his words and I can always depend on him to be brutally honest. How many of us think this same response while getting ready for church on Sunday or even bright and early during the week when sleeping in seems much better than getting ourselves to church or reading the Bible? I'm always so glad after I've spent time with God either at church or reading God's word but I will admit I can relate to my 10 year old's response.

The living room filled with the sweet, warm aroma of coffee. Three of the four kids are snoozing away and even with Isaac awake, the house is silent and still. I unlock my phone and my first instinct is to check Facebook. Facebook is really the only way I can communicate with other people but I know that I need to read my devotional first. So I reluctantly open my Bible app instead of my Facebook app and start reading. The devotional that I am currently reading was the book of Job. Job definitely puts life into perspective. He has so many things go wrong yet he clings to God and stays faithful through it all.

God communicates through his word and if you do not open your Bible sometimes then God is not going to be able to communicate with you. I find my comfort through God's word. There are so many promises that he makes but I have to seek him. I cannot complain when things are rough, if I am not seeking God's guidance. Many of the verses that I am using in this book have come from years of studying the Bible, Bible studies, and TV preachers. Seeking God can be done in many ways but I know that going straight to the Bible seems to be the quickest way to get what you need.

Finding time to read my Bible is not easy but I do it. Life is hard and busy but if you are too busy to open the Bible then you are too busy. Find the time, make the time to read your Bible or listen to a preacher. The #1 reason that I can stay content and happy in my life is because I take the time to read God's word and I take the time to talk to God everyday. He gives me strength when I cannot. He gives me peace when the storm is raging around me but if I did not take the time to seek him, I would not receive his strength and his calm.

Daily Challenge

Read your Bible. My challenge today is that you intentionally seek God even if it is just 5 minutes. Seeking God must be a priority in your life especially if you expect God to work in your life.

DAY 8
Strength

The Sovereign LORD is my strength; he makes my feet like the feet of a deer, he enables me to tread on the heights.

Habakkuk 3:19

As I sat up with my beautiful new baby girl it was 1 am. Of course she wanted to nurse again which is obviously normal but I was alone and exhausted. There's nothing like new mom tired unless you add 2 kids with autism to the mix and my husband was out of town for work and I was 3 weeks postpartum and alone. His job took him out of town a lot which left me home to fend for myself with 3 boys and my newborn. Sleep was not happening ever and my only relief was when Isaac's therapist came to the house. I did not even know that you could be as tired as I was but I kept pushing on through the exhaustion to care for my babies. A lot of people would ask how I survived but few people showed up to help. I was alone and desperately wanting just to sleep. It is hard to understand until you live it. I could not really go anywhere because Isaac would get upset if we went to the store. This is one of my favorite verses in the entire Bible because it gives me strength. During this time of my life, I would constantly pray for God's strength to get through each day. This verse gives me hope and strength to survive each day.

Even now as my daughter gets older and I am getting more sleep I still pray this verse because life still gets hard. I recently stopped working because we cannot find childcare for Isaac. Daycares have kicked him out and not a lot of people are jumping to babysit a child with special needs. It has not been easy and it has caused lots of new issues with money and conflict between my husband and I. It has been hard for me too because teaching was my dream but it has become clear that I cannot teach and raise a special needs child at the same time. God is there though. He is giving me strength to do what I need to do to care for my children and he is giving me new direction. I know that God is leading me to something great and I think that the struggles that I've experienced will help me witness to others.

Daily Challenge

What has God given you strength for? I could make a huge list of all the things that God has given me strength to overcome. I challenge you today to think of one major problem that you will face today and ask God for strength to face it. I am super concerned about having to explain that my nonverbal son cannot talk today. We have a fun event but I have a feeling that a lot of people will not know how to react to him.

DAY 9
Stay Thankful

Pray continually, give thanks in all circumstances; for this is God's will for you in Christ Jesus.
1 Thessalonians 5:17-18

Brown mud covers my son from head to toe. Not only is he covered in what I think is mud but he is completely naked. One of my eight year old's favorite games is to go outside, strip down, and play in the mud. He also really likes to squat and poop in the yard. We installed a privacy fence to not only try to contain him but to protect the neighbors from witnessing our naked, wild child taking a poop in the backyard. He is very quick too. I run in the house to change a baby diaper and when I come back out my little Houdini has managed to take off his clothes and has replaced them all with mud and probably some poo. He continues bouncing his ball around the yard trying out different terrain. He enjoys hearing the ball hit different surfaces and experiments with the sound and how it bounces back. He seems completely unaware that he is completely naked. He seems to enjoy being in his birthday suit.

I go out to ruin his fun because I know it is not okay to play outside naked and it is not okay to poop in the yard. I have Lilly (my one year old on my hip) because I am not ever allowed to sit down our little queen of the house. I yell for Isaac to come inside but of course he does not. He does look at me and even makes eye contact but then makes a little happy sound and runs to the back of the yard. So I walk down the steps and walk through the nice muddy yard to try to get the 60 lb kid to voluntarily walk into the house.

I first try some bribery.
"Isaac, do you want some grilled cheese?"
"Isaac, do you want a gummy?"
"Isaac, do you want a shower?"

I try to say all of his favorite things and I pray that something will entice him enough so I do not have to try to drag him through the yard. When he was little I could just pick him up and go. Now he is up to my shoulders and over 60 lbs. I can carry him but it is not easy and I also had my little attachment (my 1 year old daughter). Thank God, today one of the bribes worked and he goes running up the stairs to the porch. I follow quickly up the stairs. If he beats me in, I know he will redecorate the house in a nice stinky shade of brown.

This was the scene at our house at least once a week. We would go outside and the second we stopped supervising, Isaac would strip. We were never gone for more than a few minutes but Isaac was quick. When he wanted to get naked, he could strip in under 10 seconds. I don't think this ever really upset me but it was embarrassing a few times when somebody would come over or a neighbor was outside to witness the naked fun but I have learned to go with the flow when it comes to Isaac. Not much shocks or grosses me out anymore. I tend to just smile and do what I got to do.

Do I wish my child would keep his clothes on and stop pooping in the yard? Well, yeah but is that going to happen? Probably not anytime soon so we just do the best we can with the resources that we have. So what does this have to do with the Bible verse?

I have already mentioned that I constantly pray. Being an autism mom is a very lonely job. Not a lot of people want to hang out, my kids do not have friends so I talk to God a lot. I probably even look crazy sometimes because I have an all day long dialogue with God. How else would I survive life without having God to talk to?

Through my prayers, I am comforted. I receive patience and strength. I know

This also is not the type of circumstance that I think most people would be grateful for. I am very thankful for the blessings that I have been given. God gave me 4 beautiful, healthy children and a husband that works harder than anybody I've ever met in my life. I have a nice house and a nice car. I have been blessed with great schools and teachers that love my children. I am also thankful for the accomplishments that my children are making. They aren't doing the same things that normal kids do but they are growing and learning. I am grateful when Isaac says I love you before bed.

I get excited every time. I thanked God when he potty trained at 5 years old. There are so many small accomplishments that happen every day that I am thankful for.

Despite how difficult things can be sometimes, I am happy and grateful for the children that God gave me. I think sometimes as moms of autistic children we start feeling sorry for ourselves which is an easy trap to fall into but if you spend your life focusing on the accomplishments and the blessings, you will be a much happier person. You cannot be angry when you are constantly thanking God for things.

Daily Challenge

What can you be thankful for today? When you have a bad day, it is not always easy to be thankful but sometimes thanking God for the good things can make the bad not seem so big. Just spend sometime today and thank God for the good in your life.

DAY 10

For as he thinketh in his heart, so *is* he...
Proverbs 23:7

If you are walking around angry that you have a special needs child, then you will walk around angry. Being a happy mom with special needs children requires a change in attitude and outlook. You have to see things differently or you will always be miserable. One thing that helped me the most during this autism journey is to get rid of those stupid developmental charts. My kids never fit and never did what the chart says so I stopped looking all together. My focus turned to raising my kids to their highest potential not to match some chart. My heart did sink a little when I saw state test scores but then I threw those suckers in the trash and decided that some stupid test could not show you anything about my child.

My 10 year is the most unique and sometimes funny child ever. He is logical and sees the world in black and white. He is constantly asking questions and trying to learn new things.

I changed my attitude and my thoughts to focus on the good things. Like when my 8 year old wrote his name or when we successfully went to the zoo and nobody tried to run away. Staying focused on my blessings helps me stay content and thankful for what I have.

Daily Challenge

Change your attitude. Make a decision to be happy today no matter what happens. I really feel like being happy is not an emotion that we have, it is a choice we make. Every single person in the world has reasons to be sad or mad but making a conscious effort to just be happy can make all the difference. Talk to a happy person and you will learn very quickly that their life is not perfect everybody has problems. Sometimes the happiest people you meet, have the biggest problems. Sometimes, when something happens, I just say God you got this. Another thing that helps me is some good worship music. It is hard to be mad or sad, when you hear a good worship song.

DAY 11

I have told you these things, so that in me you may have peace. In this world you will have trouble. But take heart! I have overcome the world.
John 16:33

As I sit here surrounded by 10 people that are here to help my son. As a parent, I feel like they are all against me and that I must fight for my son. I know that they are here for my son but for some reason when I get into an IEP meeting I always feel ready to fight. I tense up and I get my guard up. Again, I know that the teachers are there to help but when I feel outnumbered and overwhelmed by the experts that are here. They always start off telling me all the stuff my kid sucks at. It's like look here is your son's low IQ score, his low state test scores, and his STAR test score. All of which show them that my son is not performing on grade level and I get to hear this a few times a year. Then they tell me all the help that my son will get. My autistic 10 year old is judged completely on all the stuff that he cannot do. If you ever met the kid, you would know how amazing he actually is.

He gets fixated on things and devotes all of his time to that fixation. At one point it was fans, he would walk around spinning everything and just staring at fans. Then, it was air conditioners and furnaces. Everywhere we would go he would want to go look at the furnaces or the air conditioners. I remember one time he came and told me that there was ice on our air conditioner I went out and checked and sure enough our AC unit was not working and it was frozen over. We turned it off and let it thaw out. The next day we turned it on and it worked fine for another few years before we had to replace it.

He went through a time when he loved the weather. He would obsess over the radars and his tablet had 25 weather apps so he could track any storm or weather system. We even took him to tour the local weather station.

Right now his obsession is washing machines. He spends hours watching videos about washing machines and wants to do laundry all the time. If you asked his advice on a washing machine, he could probably tell you which ones are the best and give you reasons why. I wouldn't be surprised if he could actually fix a washing machine.

I do get down and depressed after an IEP meeting but then I read a verse like this and I am reminded that Jesus conquered the world. Who cares about a stupid test score? Do you think when we get to heaven, God will be like hey I see you were novice on you state test score? Not a chance but for some reason I let this ruin my day.

To me this is one of the most empowering verses in the entire Bible. I think a lot of people assume that if you are a Christian than things should be perfect but it says right here that we will have trouble. Life is hard and everybody has problems. God promises us that we will have problems. My son's low test scores is a problem but it shouldn't define my life or his life. I believe if God can overcome death and the world than he can overcome a low test score. God has big plans for this kid whether he scores a novice or a distinguished. He is an amazing kid.

This verse also gives me strength to face each day. I think every mom has days when the kids are wearing you down and you just want to crawl in a hole and hide until bedtime. This verse gives me power to keep going. If Jesus can conquer the world, then I can surely conquer 2 hours before bedtime.

Daily Challenge

Pray to God for peace today. Find something that gives you peace. When I am feeling discontented or overwhelmed, I love to take a bath, light candles, listen to worship music, sing as loud as I can, pray, or dance. Find what gives you peace and take time to do it today.

DAY 12

Yet those who wait for the LORD Will gain new strength; they will mount up with wings like eagles, They will run and not get tired, They will walk and not become weary.
Isaiah 40:31

Our first Sunday at our new church was rough. I was all alone with four kids by myself. Isaac flipped out and started head butting me. Week two was so smooth. First of all my husband was there which always makes things a little easier because we can divide and conquer. This week he took Isaac and I had the other three little Herzogs. Isaac went right into his room with no tears and no head butting. It is moments like this when you realize how much of an autism mom you are because you get so excited about your child adjusting and happily going into the room at church that you feel like you are jumping out of your skin with excitement. I was beyond thrilled. The 3 other Herzog's also happily went to their room. I was relaxed and got to feel like a regular, normal mom. My hair and makeup stayed intact and my clothes were not disheveled. I was still together. These moments unfortunately do not happen all that often and are short lived. It gives you hope that your child might be okay and that you are doing a great job as a mom.

Then we get in the service and I swear to you the preacher was talking directly to me. He started off telling the story of Abraham and Sarah as they waited for their dream of having a child. God had promised them lots of little blessings but as they got older, it did not seem to be happening for them. They waited and waited until they decided to try to intervene and speed up God's plan. They thought that taking matters into their own hands would work out. Sarah gave Hagar to Abraham and let him impregnate her. This plan seems to backfire but eventually Sarah does get pregnant with Isaac. I do not want to go into the entire story but this is a perfect example of how we must wait on God and stop trying to rush him.

I don't know about you but I hate waiting for anything. My husband is the same way. Together, my husband and I have managed to get ourselves in and out of debt multiple times but it is because neither of us like to wait. As we get older, we have gotten much better but we are still not good at it. Part of this is because we have been raised in a world that goes 100 miles an hour all the time. There is not time to wait and be patient.

Here we are though with two autistic children and guess what, we are learning to wait. I remember praying for years that my children would talk. Jayden started talking around 4 and now he talks nonstop. Sometimes I have to remind myself that all of his talking is actually an answered prayer. Isaac started talking around five and at eight years old, he still only uses his speech for requests. On one hand, it is what I asked for because he is talking but on the other hand I want more. I want to hear what is going on in his little head. I want him to be able to tell me what is bothering him. Most of his head-butting and frustration starts because he cannot tell me why he is upset or what he needs. It is beyond frustrating but we are in a period of waiting. We are waiting for a healing miracle. We are praying for God to take away the autism. We are praying for my children to be independent adults.

We've been praying not for about seven years and asking God for healing. Along the way, we have had shimmers of hope and little miracles. I thank God for each little miracle. God is working in my boys but it is on his time not mine. While I wait, God has given me strength to continue to face our daily struggles. Bottom line though is I must wait on the Lord as he works on my children.

Daily Challenge

What are you waiting on the Lord for? I challenge you to write down your need and pray about it. Set a reminder in your phone to look at your need in a year.

I really think sometimes we pray for things and then we forget that we prayed for it. For the longest time I prayed and even fasted a few times for the financial situation so that I could stay home. Finding childcare for Isaac was getting more and more difficult and more and more expensive. I prayed for two years before the chance came along. It also came at the perfect time because we were left with no babysitting options.

DAY 13

Be still before the LORD and wait patiently for him; do not fret when people succeed in their ways, when they carry out their wicked schemes. Refrain from anger and turn from wrath; do not fret-it leads only to evil.
Psalm 37:7-8

"Tag, you're it!" screams the little blonde girl as she tags my son and runs. My son put his hands over his ears and runs the opposite way to avoid any more contact with the little girl. I feel a pang of jealousy in my gut because my son doesn't play like other children. He is a sweet, cuddly boy but has no desire to socialize with other children and he doesn't seem to understand any games. He is completely in his own little bubble. I have no idea what is going on in his head most of the time but my heart sinks when I see other kids playing normal. I feel like I am missing out on this normal life that other parents get to experience. Other parents get to hear their children talk and watch them run. Other parents get to see their children grow into adults and become independent. These are things that I do not think we will get to see with Isaac.

In this verse, I am focusing a lot on the part about waiting on the Lord and not fretting when people succeed. It takes a lot of effort not to feel down when I see other people and their normal children. Overtime, I have learned that comparing my children to others only brings me sadness. This is not the way that I want to live my life. I am choosing to love my children and trust that God is doing something amazing. I think that half the battle when you are a special needs parent is to stop trying to compare your children to others. Just because my child is different doesn't mean that God doesn't have an amazing plan for him.

I still pray that God will heal my child and now I wait for God to do his work. While I wait I have to decide every day to wake up and thank God for these beautiful children. I have thank God for the daily accomplishments and tiny miracles because that means that God hears my prayers. God is working in my life. God's time line is much different than mine and even though it seems like he is taking forever, I plan to stay focused and continue to pray and be thankful as I wait on God.

Daily Challenge

I challenge you to get rid of the developmental charts and stop trying to make your child the same as other children. I even challenge you to write a list of wonderful things that your child does that other children their age do not. Children with special needs are special and unique. Comparing them to others only makes us crazy. My son (Jayden) loves to talk and teach me about washing machines and ceiling fans. He has actually taught me a lot of new things. I do not know any other 10 year old boys that teach their parents about washing machines and fans.

DAY 14

Devote yourselves to prayer, being watchful and thankful.

Colossians 4:2

Somedays it is hard to be thankful. Life is frustrating when it does not do what you want. After a bad day of meltdowns or poop (somedays both), I find myself being thankful for cleaning supplies and running water. On good days, I am thankful for Isaac snuggles, Jayden's very honest conversations, Eli's newest Lego creation, or my Lilly bug being silly. When I look at my life, there is way more good than bad but the bad seems stronger than the good. Staying focused and keeping a positive attitude helps me stay content. It is hard to be angry, when you are thanking God and praising God.

One of the most important secrets to my happiness is prayer. I do not sit down and pray for hours but I keep a constant prayer all day long. I wake up and usually pray for a few minutes but throughout the day I pray. I pray to God like he was my best friend and so every time something happens good or bad, I am like "God, did you see that?"

I am by no means an expert but this is what works for me. I do not have a lot of time to spend in prayer so for me praying in short spurts works. It also helps me unload my struggles. When I wake up in the morning I typically do not feel as burdened but as the day goes on problems arrive. I send up my little prayers and I can let those struggles go. I can have peace because I do not walk around carrying these problems with me. I can give my struggles to God. He does not always take the problems away immediately but he always gives me peace to stay calm and strength to stand up to the problems.

Daily Challenge

I challenge you to pray more often. If you pray once a day, then I say try for at least twice a day. Do not make it into a big show or anything just say a little prayer in your head. I pray in the car, while taking walks, and even while cleaning. I make time in the mornings (when possible) to pray but sometimes it does not work. Sometimes, I have to pray when I get a chance.

<u>Day 15</u>

Do everything without grumbling or arguing Philippians 2:14

The mountains of clothes seems to double every 30 seconds. How in the world do we have so much laundry? My laundry room looks like 50 people must be living here instead of 6. The chances of me actually keeping ahead of the laundry are slim to none. In our house, we have the normal everyday clothes that you wear plus we have Isaac laundry. Isaac produces an interesting combination of pee, poop, and mud laundry. Isaac is potty trained probably 90% of the time but every other day we are washing blankets or clothes. He tends to pee on his blankets every night. I would not call it an accident since it seems to be on purpose. I have caught him in the act of just peeing on his blankets or on the carpet. He seems to like the sound of pee when it hits the carpet/blankets. We also have multiple issues with poop or as we call it "fun with feces." Then there is his dirty clothes from playing outside. The kid seems to roll around in the mud. He seems to enjoy being dirty and it is my job to try to keep him clean. I am pretty sure I fail at this job most of the time but he typically goes to school and church fairly clean.

As you can probably tell, I have a lot that I could complain about. I found this verse one day and I have no idea what I was looking for but when I saw this verse it spoke to me. It was not necessarily in a good way. It was almost like the verse was God's way of keeping me in check. He was like "Ummmm, Chrissy, I hear a lot of complaining down there." I wrote this verse on an index card and hung it right in front of the washer and dryer to remind me every single time I do laundry. I should be doing this without complaining or grumbling. God did not make us to be lazy bums. I was created to take care of my family and my kids which also means God created me to do the laundry. God created me to attempt to keep Isaac clean.

I focus this verse mostly around my least favorite job which is laundry but I have to remind myself about this one all the time. It would be so easy to walk around complaining about life. To say that my life is hard is an understatement. There are days when I am wondering "how in the world did I just survive that day?" My kids are hard, my dog is annoying, and my husband is tired. Somehow I have to try to keep everybody healthy, clean, and happy (for the most part). The best way to start doing this is to stop complaining and just do it. Do what you have to do and don't waste time complaining about how hard it is. God is there to give you strength and peace but you have to stop complaining long enough to allow God to give you these things.

Daily Challenge

Do not complain about anything for an entire day. When you feel the urge to complain, say a little prayer or turn on some good music but do not complain. Clean or cook as though you are working for God.

Day 16

We can make our plans, but the Lord determines our steps.
Proverbs 16:9

When I was five years old, I remember playing school with my siblings. I was always the teacher of course. I would make my students worksheets and make a little classroom. I knew from such a young age that I wanted to be a teacher. I worked my butt off to get there too. All the way through school, I worked so hard because I was determined to go to college and become a teacher. I had dreams of changing lives and being a spectacular teacher. I was going to win awards and my students would all love me. I did become a teacher but right from the start reality started setting in. Teaching was not at all what I expected. It was hard. I tried to plan all the fun lessons I had played in my head. The only problem is they did not work the way I planned. The students that I had did not respond like the kids in my head. After my first year of teaching, I was pink slipped because of budget cuts but I was still determined to teach so I searched and managed to get a second teaching job. It went a little better but still not at all what I imagined and then I got pink slipped again. I managed to get a few different teaching jobs. I got better at teaching but then autism hit our household.

Life got really complicated after we had our second son diagnosed with autism. At first, it wasn't too bad because he was only three. Most day cares were still willing to deal with his behavior and his delays because they weren't too far from normal. As other kids started learning and becoming preschoolers then school age children Isaac kind of stayed frozen in time. He was stuck. Developmentally, he was very similar to a two year old but he was physically getting bigger. We survived kindergarten and first grade. During second grade, he was kicked out of daycare because at this point they felt that they could no longer care for him. He was running out the front door, head butting other children, and again having lots of poop issues. We went through a few babysitters and we did find one that helped us finish off the year but she decided to not come back for the new year. So I spent the summer unsuccessfully looking for a new babysitter for him. Nobody wanted to watch him and August was coming. I was supposed to start work but nobody wanted to watch my baby boy. I just kept praying that God would find a way to make something work out.

It was the end of July when my husband was offered a new job. It was far away from our house and I would have to quit teaching but I wouldn't have to worry about childcare for him anymore. I prayed to God that he would open doors if this was meant to be. Things all started falling into place. We moved, my husband got a new job, and my entire life changed.

Here I am a stay at home mom. I never saw this coming. I never imagined that I would have to give up my teaching career to care for an autistic child. This is more proof that God is in control. I made plans to be a teacher and I tried to plan my life out, God had other plans and he is guiding my family's steps through life.

This verse proves that social media is not all bad. I was scrolling through my Facebook one day and this verse was there. I knew right away that this one has to be in this book. It is so funny to think about me making plans but at one point in my life, I attempted to make plans. The older I get, the more I realize that God is in control and not me. The older I get, the more I realize that God's ways and thoughts are so much higher than mine that I could never comprehend.

Daily Challenge

Can you think of any plans you made that were completely turned upside down by God? Are you making plans now? I challenge you to pray for God to open or close doors to help guide you to where he wants you. I prayed this before my husband took a new job and God started opening up doors like crazy. It encouraged us to make a huge move but God answered and showed us where to go.

Day 17

For we live by faith, not by sight
2 Corinthians 5:7

Living by faith is not easy especially when your life seems to be a mess. I know that I am not the only person in this world that has a rough life. Every single person in this world has problems and every single person at some point in their life feels like their life is the hardest life. Everybody's problem seems like the worst problem in the world. My problem is autism and all of the craziness that having a child with autism brings to a family. Having a child with autism changes everything and impacts every single part of my world, my husband's world, and my other children's world. In some ways, we all have to adjust our lives for autism.

I think living life by faith is hard because we are unable to see or understand why we face struggles. I have questioned God about why I have 2 children with autism and why my life cannot just be normal. I think the hardest thing is the fact that my son cannot tell me what is wrong and he doesn't call me mom. I think every mom dreams of the day their child says mom but for me I am still waiting on my eight year old to say mom. It is hard breaking and I have no idea why God does not just use his power to fix my son.

The thing is that I do not know what God's plan is. God has a plan so much bigger than my understanding. Learning to walk by faith has been one of the toughest things I have ever learned to do. I had to stop trying to understand why my children are autistic and I had to learn that God is in control. God has a plan. We are not meant to understand everything in our life, we are made to trust God. I have concluded that I cannot be happy and live my life questioning and worrying about things that I cannot change. When I feel myself worrying or starting to question, I delve into my Bible or I turn on a preacher. I know that leaning on God and depending on his word are the best ways to help me walk by faith. Stop trying to depend on your own understanding, lean on God and you can live an imperfect content life.

Daily Challenge

I challenge you to try walking by faith. I feel like when we worry about a problem, we are saying that we do not trust that God will take care of it, so I challenge you to stop worrying about something. Easier said than done but start small. I challenge you to give God a problem today and then let him have it. Every Time, you think about it or start worrying about it, find a way to seek God. Either pray, journal, read your Bible, or turn on a Christian song.

Day 18

God is our refuge and strength, an ever-present help in trouble
Psalm 46:1-3

Dinner in the oven finally, baby on my hip, and there is Isaac pooping right beside the front door. For the life of me, I cannot figure out why this kid will plop down and poop anywhere except the toilet. I grab him and run him up to the shower but not before he smears poop all over the wall and on my blankets. I sit the baby down and she of course starts screaming her brains out because there are certain times of night where she does not like to be set down. I wrestle with Isaac to get him undressed and he giggles because apparently pooping in the yard is fun. Lilly continues to scream and then the oven timer starts going off. My 10 year old runs upstairs and yells “Mommy mommy, the timer is going off!” I run downstairs, stop the timer, pull out dinner while blocking the oven so the baby doesn’t try to touch it, then I pick up Lilly and run back upstairs to check on Isaac in the shower. As soon as I walk into my room, I smell more poop. Isaac of course has decided to poop all over the shower and rub it in his hair. So I get him out of the shower and of course he wants to stay in so he sits down in the poop. I finally manage to get him into the bath so I can clean the shower floor (while still holding the baby on my hip).

I am going to stop there because you get the idea. Now repeat this story seven days a week and you have my life. I am kidding. Isaac does not poop in the front yard every day but there are always 20 different things that I am trying to deal with at one time and usually Isaac is one of them. Whether it is a poop issues, him demanding grilled cheese or chocolate milk, or asking for his favorite show, it is always something. Isaac has no patience. He usually will ask for something once before he starts getting frustrated with you. Usually, he is okay asking a second time but at some point he starts getting violent because you are not doing what he wants at an acceptable speed. It is extremely hard to explain patience to a child with limited communication skills. On a normal day, he says one of four things either I want grilled cheese, chocolate milk, Yo Gabba Gabba, or Wonder Pets. Occasionally we will get “I want outside” or “I want bye bye.” My life is hard and I do not think anybody would disagree with me. Most people do not understand the extent to how hard it is but nobody would say I have been given an easy life. Most people are shocked that I am happy and that I still make an effort to have fun with my kids. I teach them new games, we play, we do crafts, and we go places even vacations. I refuse to sit back and have a pity party but it is hard.

The way that I chose to face each day is through God. He is my rock. He is the one I can cling to when my kids are making me crazy. He is the one who knows exactly what I am dealing with and I cling to him. My best advice to anybody facing special needs is to pray often and surround yourself with Godly things. I know how hard it is to sit and read the Bible but it is possible to turn on Christian radio. You can ask my kids because I sing it loud. I praise God driving down the road, making dinner, and cleaning house. I also think that watching preachers. I turn on a preacher while I clean. It is hard to sit still when you live a life with special needs children but surrounding yourself with strength helps equip you to face anything every single day. I find that equipping myself with

God's word and praising him throughout the day gives me strength to not only face the day but to be able to find joy even in the roughest circumstances.

Daily Challenge

I challenge you to read your Bible every day for a week even if it is one verse a day, read the Bible. You cannot expect God to give you strength, if you do nothing to seek him. You cannot expect God to give you strength, if you are not equipping yourself. So seek God everyday by reading your Bible.

<u>**Day 19**</u>

I know what it is to be in need, and I know what it is to have plenty. I have learned the secret of being content in any and every situation, whether well fed or hungry, whether living in plenty or in want. I can do all this through him who gives me strength. Philippians 4:12-13

I will admit that I have never gone hungry. There were days when I remember having limited food options but we always had something to eat. We definitely did not live with excess growing up but I remember feeling content. I always felt like safe and I always felt like my parents would ensure that I had everything that I needed. I knew that we were not well off but I was happy because I was loved.

I think having a relationship with God is similar in many ways to our earthly families. Sometimes, things are not perfect and sometimes you feel like you do not have what you want but you can be content because you know that somebody is going to make it okay. You feel content because you know that you will not go hungry and you know that you will have what you need. The Lord is our strength and our provider which makes it possible for us to be content even when faced with daily struggles.

Everybody has their daily struggles and their problems. I am not going hungry and I cannot think of many material things that I really want that I cannot go and purchase but I do live my life in want. I think a lot of people live their life wanting something or being hungry for something. My want is to have children without autism. I want my children to be normal, talk, make friends, play sports, and be able to do normal kid stuff. I want to know that my boys will be able to grow up, get jobs, get married, move out, and have children. I want my children to be self-sufficient. I want to be able to go to the grocery store without it being a huge issue. I want to be able to take my kids out to eat or go to a museum. I want to see my children succeed in life. I could go on and on of all the things that I want but that would require another book.

The part that I love about this verse is where it says despite all of this I have found the secret to being content. What??? How many self-help books are out there about the secret to being happy? Well here it is summed up in one sentence. The secret to being happy and content despite your circumstance is through Jesus Christ. I can do all things through Jesus Christ who gives me strength.

Now to clarify that, this does not mean that God is magic genie in a bottle that will do what you want, this means that God is there to strengthen you through the hard times. God promises us in John 16:33 that we will have problems in this world so we know that things are not and will not be perfect but we can lean on God to strengthen us and we can be content in any circumstance if we lean on God.

How do you lean on God when times are hard? Read the Bible, pray, worship, and fellowship. In order for God to give you strength, you have to equip yourself to face the devil. The only way to equip yourself is to connect yourself with God. The best way to do this is to read the Bible. The Bible is your life line and it is packed full of promises and Bible verses that you can lean on when things are no good.

Daily Challenge

Be happy! Write a list of things that you have to be happy about. Thank God for those things. Focus on those things and worship God.

Day 20

Working for God

Whatever you do, work at it with all your heart, as working for the Lord, not for human masters
Colossians 3:23

I recently quit my job to stay home with my kids. It was not necessarily the dream job I had in mind. It was not the plan but it has become my life. My kids have taken over my world and so my dream of being a teacher has been put on the back burner. I am not saying that I will never go back to teaching but it does not make sense right now. My husband's job is very demanding and so I feel that I need to be here to pick up the slack.

So here I am with a Master's Degree in Education but I am cleaning toilets, washing dishes, changing diapers, cooking dinner, and all of the other chores that go along with keeping up with a household full of kids. Not exactly what you would expect from somebody that went to college for 6 plus years and graduated with an almost perfect GPA. One thing I have realized over the years that it really does not matter what your job is. God sees us all the same but whatever you are doing you should be doing it as though God was your boss.

When I clean my bathroom, I am cleaning it for God. When I change that stinky diaper, I am doing it for God. When you believe that you are working for God, it changes how you look at your job and how you do your job. Yes, I am a stay at home mom to two autistic children and two typical children. Yes, this job doesn't pay but I am putting my all into it because I am working for God. God is my boss and God is the one that I want to please. So even though parts of this job seem below some people, I know that I am doing this for God not for men. I am raising my children for God, I am cleaning my house for God, and I am supporting my husband for God.

As an autism parent, there are extra responsibilities but when I realize that I am caring for this beautiful child of God, it changes how you do it. God entrusted me to care for these boys and God has a purpose for my boys so my job is to do everything in my power to take care of their needs and help them become men of God. When you are working for God, you put your whole heart into it even if some people see your job as less important.

Daily Challenge

Are you doing your job like you would if Jesus was your boss? The next time you go to work, work for God. If you are flipping burgers, then cook them like it is for God. If you are cleaning toilets, then clean the toilet like Jesus is going to use it. If you are a teacher, teach like you would if Jesus was your principal. It does not matter what your job is, just spend the day doing your job like God was your boss or your customer. How would you do your job different?

Day 21

Have I not commanded you? Be strong and courageous. Do not be afraid; do not be discouraged, for the LORD your God will be with you wherever you go."
Joshua 1:9

There are many times in my life when I do not feel good enough. I feel like no matter what I do, it is not good enough. I feel discouraged and like a failure. I feel pressured to meet unrealistic expectations from all directions. At the end of the day, I just feel like I am failing at everything. I am not skinny enough, I do not make enough money, I cannot keep my house clean, I am not a good mom, I am not a good wife, and the list could go on and on. I believe the devil is behind these unrealistic expectations. I have to trust in God and I have to stop trying to meet unrealistic expectations of the world.

For some reason I have been struggling a lot lately with this. I think it hits harder when the unrealistic expectations come from the people closest to you. When somebody makes you feel like crap because you are not as skinny as you were before 4 children or somebody that makes you feel bad because you really cannot do it all. For some reason moms nowadays are expected to do everything. We still have responsibilities to care for the house, take care of our children but now we are also supposed to try to work and make money. On top of all of that I have 2 children with autism.

My eight year old has the kind of autism that people are scared of. He is not a super genius or Rainman like television likes to portray. He is not verbal. He head-butts, wanders off, makes weird sounds, and plays in his poop. We are at the point in his life where people no longer want to babysit him. We used to have support when he was little and his behavior was more acceptable. Now he is eight and guess what almost nobody is left to help us out. We have no babysitters and respite care through the state does not pay anybody enough to watch him. I cannot do it all and I definitely cannot do it alone.

I pray to God for some relief. I pray to God that the people around me will start to understand. I pray to God for courage and strength to continue living my life with little to no support. I need God to survive the life of being an autism mom. I cannot do it alone. God is with me wherever I go. With God's help, I can thrive in this life I've been given. I am not perfect and I will make mistakes but I am trusting that God has a plan for me. I am giving it all to him because I have no clue what I am doing. I am giving it all to him because I have no clue how my story will end. I just pray and ask God to take the struggles so that I can be content in my life.

I get discouraged in my life. I get frustrated and I get tired. I love knowing that God will be with me every step of the way. There are so many verses and stories in the Bible of God being with people through their struggles. When I get discouraged, this is one way that I can stay strong. I am also a person that loves music so for me turning on some worship music and singing my heart out to the Lord helps a lot. It is hard to stay discouraged and frustrated, when you are praising God.

Daily Challenge

Turn on some worship music and praise God. In my experience, one of the best way to feel strengthened by God is to praise him.

Day 22

He is the one you praise; he is your God, who performed for you those great and awesome wonders you saw with your own eyes.
Deuteronomy 10:21

We planned a weekend trip to visit some of my family in Mississippi. I was pretty excited but very concerned too. Traveling with two autistic children can be tricky. My husband and I never let this hold us back because we enjoy going to new places so we push through and plan as well as we can for any possible troubles. My grandma lives out in the country so there are no hotels so we booked ourselves a cabin at a camping ground. The cabin was right by a lake. Most people would think that this was great...lake view cabin but this scared me to no end. Isaac loves water and he loves swimming. He has jumped into lakes before with no sense of danger or temperature.

My mind obviously goes to the worst case scenario, Isaac gets out of the cabin while we are sleeping and goes for a swim. I prayed when I booked it and I prayed a lot on the way there that Isaac would not try to jump in on us.

We arrive and the weekend honestly went perfect. Isaac did not even try to jump into the lake. He walked around, explored, and bounced his ball but no jumping. He also did not have any accidents, no poop issues, and no meltdowns. I went an entire weekend without getting head-butted. You better bet I am thanking God for a peaceful, successful weekend!

Now, not everybody sees this as a miracle but I definitely think this is a miracle. For some reason, people only look for big miracles instead of focusing on all of the little miracles around us. We live in a beautiful world, if you really look at it. While we were at the cabin, I sat outside in the morning and watched the sunrise (another perk of having an autistic child). All I could think, while watching the sunrise over this big lake, is that I serve an awesome God. He has created miracles and beauty all around us. The birds, the sky, the rain, the sunrise, and yes my son having an awesome weekend. This was the first weekend that I have felt relaxed in a long time. My husband and I even were able to sit on the porch after the kids went to bed and we got to talk.

Daily Challenge

I would challenge anybody reading this book to take a minute and look for miracles around you. God is good and God is performing miracles everywhere, we just have to slow down and look. We are so busy with our cell phones and so busy trying to do too much that we miss God's miracles. I promise if you stop and look, you will start to see God's miracles all around you.

Day 23

As iron sharpens iron, so one person sharpens another.
Proverbs 27:17

It's 7 am and the phone rings. It is my best friend. She calls me every single morning to talk on her way to work. This call usually comes after I get two kids off to school and I have two left at home. I love our morning calls because I can complain, brag, laugh, and tell stories to another adult. Since I quit working to stay home with my kids, my life pretty much revolves around my kids. I am in no way complaining because I am so thankful that I can stay home but I love my morning talks with my best friend. She gives me strength and confidence. She listens and comforts. She gives advice or suggestions. She is the iron that sharpens me. Everybody needs a person like this in their life.

Being a parent of children with special needs is lonely. My children do not make friends, they do not play sports, and they do not socialize. On top of that, it is difficult to go anywhere with my boys. When we do go places such as the park, I cannot sit and talk to other moms because my son is a flight risk. If I turn my back or walk away, there is a good chance he will be gone.

I have found a few ways to make friends. One is through church. Now this depends a lot on your church, your spouse, and any other support you might have. I was lucky enough to find a church when we lived in Kentucky that provided childcare for my children with special needs. They even had a group dedicated to special needs parents that provided childcare when they met. You cannot get much better than that. Even then it was hard to attend because if Isaac had a bad day, I was not about to torture everybody by forcing him to leave the house.

My husband has also been a huge support in helping me make friends. He has worked his work schedule so that I can go to small groups and meet up with friends. He is flexible and encouraging.

Finding friends and putting yourself out there is hard. I have to force myself sometimes to be social and to do things that I really do not want to do because I know it is good for me. I know that I need friends but it is easier sometimes to stay home and become a hermit.

You need friends especially when you are on the path as an autism parent. Being a special needs parent should not be done alone. You need people to be there for encouragement and laughter.

Daily Challenge

I have 2 challenges for you today.
One is to pray that God will bring people into your life (not on Facebook) that can be there to support you and your walk with God.
My second challenge is to talk to somebody new.

Day 24

Shout for joy to the LORD, all the earth. Worship the LORD with gladness; come before him with joyful songs. Know that the LORD is God. It is he who made us, and we are his; we are his people, the sheep of his pasture. Enter his gates with thanksgiving and his courts with praise; give thanks to him and praise his name. For the LORD is good and his love endures forever; his faithfulness continues through all generations.
Psalm 100

Three am and my one year old daughter keeps waking me up. She is so needy sometimes. It is probably my fault but she wants to sleep with me every night and she wakes up multiple times a night to make sure that I have not moved. She is not a good sleeper and again it is probably my fault for not pushing her into her bed before now. The lack of sleep stinks but I know it won't last forever. I look at my oldest son who is 10 years old and he never jumps in bed to cuddle with me. It would honestly be a little weird if he did but I remember cuddling him when he was a tiny baby. Kids grow out of wanting to cuddle and kids grow out of wanting to sleep in your bed. Babies grow up so I am kind of embracing my last baby even though she causes me to lose sleep.

It is 3 am and I am tired but I cannot sleep so I decided to start writing and researching more for my book. I came across this chapter in the Bible and I had to include it because even in my tired state, this verse uplifted me. Sometimes when things are hard, reading a verse that encourages happiness and worship is exactly what you need. Life is hard.

This verse says it all. Praise God, give thanks to God, and his love and faithfulness will always be there. This is not always easy to read when things are not going well but when I read this I feel uplifted and hopeful. This makes me want to raise my hands up and sing. This makes me want to thank God for my life and my blessings.

When I am going through a hard time, the quickest way to brighten my mood is to sing praises to God and be thankful. I know I have said this before but it really is hard to be in a bad mood when you are singing and praising God. I tend to make a joyful noise to God instead a joyful song but it doesn't matter God hears it whether it sounds good or terrible.

Daily Challenge

I challenge you to sing and praise God today. I think I have said this many times but find some good worship music and today you need to sing loud. Make a joyful noise and praise God. I like to do this while I clean, shower, or even when I am driving. Find a place and sing praises to God.

Day 25

Supporting Others

Praise be to the God and Father of our Lord Jesus Christ, the Father of compassion and the God of all comfort, who comforts us in all our troubles, so that we can comfort those in any trouble with the comfort we ourselves receive from God.

2 Corinthians 1:3-4

"My son is not talking, does he have autism?"

"How do I get services? What did you do?"

"What would you do if Isaac won't take a bath?"

"How did you potty train?"

These are just a few examples of questions that I have gotten over the years. Since becoming an autism mom 7 years ago, I have learned a lot about special needs. I have learned about potty training special needs children, advocating for my kids at school, IEPs, state waivers, speech therapy, occupational therapy, stimming, and so many more fun special needs information. As I learned, I would constantly share on social media and with friends about the different obstacles that I was facing. At first, it was to vent my frustrations. I think every special needs parent gets frustrated because it is so hard to do anything. Nothing in our world is easy and everything takes too long.

The thing I did not realize though is that as I was posting and sharing my experiences, other people were facing similar issues. The questions started coming and before I knew, I think people thought I was an expert (which I am not). I started getting questions from friends, coworkers, and family members that were concerned for their own child or that were facing problems. I soon realized that I could use the hurdles that we were facing to help other people facing the same obstacles.

This verse really stopped me in my tracks when I found it because I hadn't really thought about the fact that I am giving comfort to others by helping them. God gives me peace and comfort during my struggles and I have been able to pass this on to others who are facing the same thing. God has given me the strength to be the mom that I was made to be. I have had days where I feel sorry for myself but how does that really help? Instead I chose to praise God for what I have and to hopefully be able to use my experience to uplift somebody else.

I also hope that through this book I can offer some peace and hope to others that are facing special needs. It is not an easy road to travel and it is easy to give in to negativity and to feel sorry for yourself. Being able to offer support to others makes me feel like I am doing something positive with this not so good hand that I have been dealt.

Daily Challenge

God gives you comfort so how can you offer comfort to someone else facing a similar situation?

Day 26

Indeed, we felt we had received the sentence of death. But this happened that we might not rely on ourselves but on God, who raises the dead.
2 Corinthians 1:9

"Is that the color you picked?" I say to my husband with a look of disgust on my face. I tend to get on his case sometimes before he is actually able to complete a task. He definitely gave me a mean look and told me to wait until it dries. He also reassures me that we can repaint if I do not like it but I have to wait for it to dry because it will look better. After a few hours, the color has dried and it looks pretty good.

I don't know about you but this tends to be a common occurrence in my house. Not just with me but with my kids too. We tend to look at an incomplete project and assume we do not like it before it is even finished. I feel that this is also how we approach our life sometimes. Things are hard and they do not look the way that we want so we start to complain. I know God has to be up there saying "would you all just calm down and let me finish?" It is hard to be patient and trust that God is doing something great when all we see is an incomplete project.

Obviously, having an autistic child is not the same as a death sentence. When you first get the news though, it kind of feels like a death sentence. You make these plans for your child and then in a few doctor's visits, you plan is annihilated. Believe me I know all too well what it is like to plan and then have your plans go up in smoke. I have had to mourn the dream of having a "perfect" child and I have had to learn to accept a completely different life.

Through my experience though, I have learned to rely on God. Things will never be perfect and every single person is facing some challenge but God is there to offer us comfort and hope. We must rely on him to do his job. We must trust that he is going to complete this job and stop complaining that it doesn't fit into our vision. God has a plan much larger than all of us. If we spend our time looking at the incomplete project, we will live our life disappointed because an incomplete project is messy and unorganized but once it is finished it will be great. Trust that God is working on a masterpiece.

Daily Challenge

Write a list of things that you can trust God for. Pray for these things but also pray for strength to accept when things do not look the way that you want.

<u>**Day 27**</u>

Not only so, but we also glory in our sufferings, because we know that suffering produces perseverance; perseverance, character; and character, hope. And hope does not put us to shame, because God's love has been poured out into our hearts through the Holy Spirit, who has been given to us.
Romans 5:3-5

I watch Isaac bounce his ball in a big puddle and then rub the ball over his mouth. He loves to run things over his lips. Nobody's quite sure why but we know it is a sensory thing. He bounces the ball right in the mud and rubs it right on his face again. He is already covered in bright red Georgia mud and on top of that he is now soaked from the puddles. I know he is having fun but I decide to bring him in because it is getting colder outside. The last thing you want is a sick autistic child.

I go out the door to get him but as soon as the door shuts, my 1 year old starts crying "momma momma momma!" I am no longer allowed to leave the room when she is awake. I firmly grab his hand and encourage him to come in the house so we can get him in the shower. He walks with me pretty easily (this is not always the case). When we walk in, Lilly is still crying so I pick her up, Isaac of course covers his ears and runs for the stairs. While this is happening, Jayden spills milk and starts screaming then Eli starts saying “Mommy, come read my sentences that I wrote!” Okay, so I start trying to deal with one problem at a time. I help Jayden clean up the milk, tell Eli to wait a minute, all while hauling Lilly around on my hip, and praying that Isaac is not making a mess (even though I know he is). I walk to the computer and look at Eli’s spelling sentences, then I bolt up the stairs while still hauling around my 20 pound kid. When I get up there of course Isaac is on my bed rolling around. Mud is all over and now there is even more to do. So I get him in the shower and wash the blankets (all while still carrying the baby). Then Jayden runs up freaking out because I started the washer while the shower was going. Apparently, that is not allowed. By the time the kids go to bed, momma is tired from running and putting out fires all day.

Being a mom to four kids is hard work but when two of them have autism the workload becomes even harder. It is seriously nonstop. I am the most needed person in my house. As soon as I finish cleaning one mess, there is something else waiting for me to do. It is hard to really describe this. It is hard to imagine that all of this will make me stronger especially since at the end of the day I feel like I have been run over by a semi-truck.

We've have all heard the saying "What doesn't kill you makes you stronger." Apparently, it is from the Bible. This verse is basically saying that when we suffer we are building perseverance, character, and hope. I look at my life and I know that I wouldn't be who I am today if it weren't for our struggles. My struggles are the reason that I am the person that I have become. My struggles are the reason that I have complete trust in God. I get up every day and I know that God is there to help me through the day. My autism journey is far from over so I have to keep going and keep fighting. Through all of this I am building perseverance and I am building hope in God.

Daily Challenge

Think about the struggles in your life that have made you stronger. Write down a few ways that your struggles have helped you become the person you are today.

Day 28

In the same way, let your light shine before others, so that they may see your good works and give glory to your Father who is in heaven.

Matthew 5:16

I constantly get asked how I do what I do. I am a mom to four awesome children. Two of my children have autism (one is very low functioning). My husband works a lot but I truly believe and trust that God has a plan for my life. Just through knowing and understanding that there is a purpose for my suffering helps me stay positive and strong.

I want to live my life to glorify God. When people ask me how I do it, I say I don't, God does it. God is the reason that I am strong and happy. God does it all. I want people to look at my life and realize that I serve an awesome God. I want people to look at my life and think "wow that God of hers makes her strong." I do not take credit for being strong or for caring for my kids and being a good mom because it is all

God's doing. I am a living example of God's power and God's miracles.

Every single day, I witness God's amazing works through my children. I watch my nonverbal son say words or eat a new food that he wouldn't eat before. I watch my beautiful daughter talk and wave bye bye which is a miracle to me. I watch my oldest son thrive into this awesome little boy and overcome all odds. My life is a beautiful example of God's work so when you look at it and wonder "how does she do it?" Just remember I don't. Without God's hand, I would be lost.

Daily Challenge

My goal in life is to live so that others see Christ in me. Try living today as though you were somebody's sermon for the day. This does not mean you have to go preach because I do not preach but I live my life with God in control. I do not have to go preaching because people can see God in my life.

<u>Day 29</u>

You will keep in perfect peace those whose minds are steadfast, because they trust in you.
Isaiah 26:3

There was a time when my mind was full of worry, fear, and anger. These emotions consumed my life so much and seemed to overhaul my life. Living in worry, fear, and anger was not what God wanted for us but it seems to be more and more common. It did not take long before it hit me that I had fallen from God. This was after trying to fix all of my problems but one day I realized I could not solve my problems. Problems were bigger than me. I will admit this did not happen overnight. It started with finding a church, then multiple failed small groups and some successful ones too, and then finally realizing that the only way for complete peace was to have complete trust in God by having a steadfast mind.

What exactly does it mean to have a steadfast mind? I actually looked up the definition on Google to get a definition.

According to Google steadfast means "resolutely or dutifully firm and unwavering." The part that stands out to me is the dutifully firm. To be dutifully firm to me would mean that you are seeking God at every chance that you can. Dutifully firm to me is reading your Bible, praying to God, and worshipping God. So many people expect God to do things and be there for them but they do not make time for God. For example if you have a friend that you stop talking but then you expect them to be there assisting you in your hard times even though you stopped being their friend. I feel like this is sort of how it works with God. Now God is there all of the time but to have this perfect peace, you have to seek God.

I am not saying that seeking God has solved all of my problems. My life is hard. My life is a mess but I am at peace with it. I am content. I trust God and I know he is doing something amazing.

So how do you find time to seek God so that you have a steadfast mind? You make the time for God. I have four kids and I make the time so I believe most people can do this too. My Bible reading time is not always at the same time. I try to do it every morning but with autistic children and a 1 year old their wake up time is unpredictable. There are some mornings when I am up at 3 am with Isaac. On those mornings, the morning Bible study doesn't work but other mornings I can get 30 minutes to an hour of time to myself to read. It really just depends on Isaac. On the days when he gets up crazy early, I find other times to squeeze in my Bible time. Sometimes, I can turn on his favorite TV show and do my Bible reading and some days I find myself trying to finish a chapter while lying in bed. It is not always ideal but I manage to read at least one chapter from the Bible every day. For me this means replacing my Facebook time or my time playing mobile games time but I make it happen every day because it is important. God is my lifeline.

I go to church almost every single Sunday. I think keeping a steadfast mind means you need to be in church, you need to worship, fellowship, and hear the sermon. Having children with special needs is a barrier to church but I have managed to find 2 churches in 2 different states that have worked with us. The first church we went to actually started their special needs program because of my son. We started it. My eight year old son with low functioning autism is the reason that kids every week are getting to hear the word of God and parents who could never attend church are able to attend church. Make it happen.

Worship for me also happens at home on a daily basis. A lot of my worship comes when I clean. I turn up that some worship music and praise God the entire time. Worship happens in my car. Every time I get in I turn up and I honestly sing my heart out. It is not always pretty but it is how I keep my mind at peace.

When I start slipping, I can feel anxiety and worry start to invade my mind. The devil is out there waiting for me to slip and he is right there ready to pounce the second that I fall away from God. Once you slip and start skipping church or stop reading your Bible, starting back again is twice as hard. Ultimately, the way to a peaceful mind even in tough times is to seek God every chance you can. Make it priority despite your circumstances. I promise you it is worth it.

Daily Challenge

Have your own worship time. Find a local Christian radio station or look up K Love and praise God.

Day 30

His disciples asked him, "Rabbi, who sinned, this man or his parents, that he was born blind?"

"Neither this man nor his parents sinned," said Jesus, "but this happened so that the works of God might be displayed in him.

John 9:2-3

"Mommy, I want to go to STEAM night!" Eli says in his whiniest little voice. This will be a disaster but letting my 6 year old down is not an option either so we load up. 4 kids in Ronda the Honda all buckled up and ready to go. For the entire 2 minute drive, I just keep praying that STEAM night will be a success. The first thing we walk into is a line. Autism and lines do not mix! Isaac drops to the floor and cries, "Go bye bye."

I push through anyway. No we are going to make it for Eli. Eli will get to have fun at STEAM night like all the other normal kids. Mommy guilt always kicks in when my neurotypical child has to miss things because of his autistic brother. We successfully made it 45 minutes before Isaac made the executive decision that he was done. Forty five minutes for Isaac was some kind of miracle but we did it.

Mommy guilt is a real thing. When you have two children with autism, there is a lot of mommy guilt. You feel guilty for your neurotypical children that miss out on things and you feel bad for your autistic child because you want them to be included in things. No matter what you do, you feel guilty. You also start wondering what in the world you did to deserve this life.

I love this verse because Jesus makes it clear that it is not my fault that I have an autistic child. I did not do anything to deserve it. He also makes it clear that I should not be living my life angry that my children have a disability but instead I should use obstacle to show how great God is. I am not saying that God caused the autism but trouble in our life is used to glorify God.

We should be living our life to glorify God. When things are hard, we lean on God. We live our life so that other people look at it and wonder how we are doing it. The name of this book is the exact question that I want to hear because it means that I am doing the impossible by overcoming obstacles that others see as too big through Jesus Christ.

Daily Challenge

Live today to glorify God. When good things happen, thank God. When bad things happen, give it to God and let it go. Live life so that people start wondering how you are doing it?

Made in United States
Troutdale, OR
06/19/2025